Family Math Night:
Middle School Math Standards in Action

Jennifer Taylor-Cox, Ph.D.
Christine Oberdorf

EYE ON EDUCATION
6 DEPOT WAY WEST, SUITE 106
LARCHMONT, NY 10538
(914) 833-0551
(914) 833-0761 fax
www.eyeoneducation.com

Library of Congress Cataloging-in-Publication Data

Taylor-Cox, Jennifer.
Family math night : middle school math standards in action / Jennifer
Taylor-Cox, Christine Oberdorf.
    p. cm.
ISBN 1-59667-028-2
1. Mathematics--Study and teaching (Middle school)--Activity programs.
2. Mathematics--Study and teaching (Middle school)--United States.
3. Education--Parent participation. I. Oberdorf, Christine. II. Title.
QA135.6.T355 2006
510.71'2--dc22   2006013781

Book design services provided by
Jennifer Osterhouse Graphic Design
3752 Danube Drive, Davidsonville, MD 21035
(410-798-8585)

Also available from Eye On Education

Family Math Night: Math Standards in Action
Jennifer Taylor-Cox

A Collection of Performance Tasks and Rubrics:
Primary School Mathematics
Charlotte Danielson and Pia Hansen Powell

A Collection of Performance Tasks and Rubrics:
Upper Elementary School Mathematics
Charlotte Danielson

A Collection of Performance Tasks and Rubrics:
Middle School Mathematics
Charlotte Danielson

A Collection of Performance Tasks and Rubrics:
High School Mathematics
Charlotte Danielson and Elizabeth Marquez

Bringing the NCTM Standards to Life:
Best Practices for Middle Schools
Yvelyne Germain-McCarthy

Bringing the NCTM Standards to Life:
Exemplary Practices from High Schools
Yvelyne Germain-McCarthy

Mathematics and Multi-Ethnic Students:
Exemplary Practices
Yvelyne Germain-McCarthy & Katharine Owens

Teaching Mathematics in the Block
Susan Gilkey and Carla Hunt

Assessment in Middle and High School Mathematics:
A Teacher's Guide
Daniel Brahier

About the Authors

 Dr. Jennifer Taylor-Cox is an energetic, captivating presenter and well-known educator. She is the Executive Director of **Innovative Instruction: Connecting Research and Practice in Education**. Jennifer serves as an educational consultant for numerous districts across the United States. Her workshops and keynote speeches are always high-energy and insightful. She earned her Ph.D. from the University of Maryland and was awarded the "Outstanding Doctoral Research Award" from the University of Maryland and the "Excellence in Teacher Education Award" from Towson University. She currently serves as the president of the Maryland Council of Teachers of Mathematics. Jennifer truly understands how to connect research and practice in education. Her passion for mathematics education is alive in her work with students, parents, teachers, and administrators. Dr. Taylor-Cox lives and has her office in Severna Park, Maryland. She is the mother of three children.

 Ms. Christine Oberdorf is a dedicated and experienced educator. She works as a Math Content Coach with Montgomery County Public Schools in Maryland, in addition to working as a consultant. She earned a M.Ed. from the University of Maryland, and currently serves as a regional representative for the Maryland Council of Teachers of Mathematics. Christine appreciates opportunities to enable educators to empower young mathematicians. Ms. Oberdorf lives in Arnold, Maryland with her husband and two children.

If you would like to have Jennifer Taylor-Cox or Christine Oberdorf present on Family Math Night at your school or if you would like to schedule professional development opportunities for educators and/or parents, please contact **Innovative Instruction: Connecting Research and Practice in Education**.

Jennifer Taylor-Cox, Ph.D., Educational Consultant, Office: 410-729-5599, Fax: 410-729-3211
Email: Jennifer@Taylor-CoxInstruction.com
Email: Christine@Taylor-CoxInstruction.com

Acknowledgments

In memory of Joseph W. Cox.

Sincere appreciation is expressed to an extraordinary team of reviewers. Thank you for your acute insight, expert content knowledge, and dedication to mathematics education.

Edward C. Nolan	Mathematics Department Chair Albert Einstein High School
Marci Goldman-Frye, M.S.	Mathematics Specialist Montgomery County Public Schools
Gail Kaplan, Ph.D.	Mathematics Department Towson University
Kira Hamman	Instructor Mathematics Department Hood College

Extensive knowledge and gratitude are offered to the thousands of students and parents who have taken part in our Family Math Night activities over the years.

Jennifer Taylor-Cox

Christine Oberdorf

Jennifer Osterhouse, Book Design

Marida Hines, Illustration

Table of Contents

Permission is granted to photocopy the pages in this book for your school's Family Math Night.

Chapter One:
Introduction

Why Should Our School Have Family Math Night?

The goal of Family Math Night is to strengthen the mathematical aptitudes of students through the power of family interaction. By sponsoring Family Math Night, educators are encouraging parents and students to appreciate the energy and pleasure of mathematics. Each activity is designed to promote mathematical thinking and communication. The hands-on approach presented in this book helps make learning mathematics a meaningful and productive process for all involved.

Parents play an important role in the academic lives of students. By participating in Family Math Night, parents can serve as models of motivation, persistence, and competency to their children. The directions for each activity are presented in a clear, concise manner,

allowing parents to guide students to a more complete understanding of various mathematics concepts. At the same time, parents may be acquiring new knowledge and solidifying or revising previous knowledge about mathematics. You may hear parents saying, "I never really understood that concept until I tried this activity," or "I never knew math could be so much fun!" In many ways, the Family Math Night activities enlighten parents as they begin to understand and value mathematics in new ways.

The concepts presented in each Family Math Night activity will help students learn essential new skills and/or reinforce skills already learned in mathematics. While working through math problems in a textbook is one way for some students to learn mathematics, there are other more interactive means of gaining knowledge of mathematics, such as the math stations presented in this book. To help realize a vision of increased math proficiency for all, we need to encourage students to think about and apply mathematics in the real world. Family Math Night can help students and parents become mathematically fulfilled and empowered!

How is *Family Math Night: Middle School Math Standards in Action* Organized?

Family Math Night: Middle School Math Standards in Action contains seven chapters. The first chapter addresses the goals and intentions of this book. Chapters two through six present math stations for the five math content standards: number and operations; algebra; geometry; measurement; and data analysis and probability. The final chapter provides additional tools for the successful implementation of Family Math Night.

Each math station has two pages. The first page offers a list of the materials needed for the station, helpful hints, answers, and math standards in action. The second page offers the directions, questions parents can ask, and a challenge. The first page is for educators to review and use to prepare each station. The second page can be photocopied and displayed at the Family Math Night station. The directions page can be laminated and mounted. Some educators find it helpful to attach each direction sheet to a file folder. The opened folder can be placed vertically at each station. Other educators prefer to place the direction sheets into display stands or onto display boards. In either case, the point is to have the directions clearly displayed at each station.

How are the Activities Connected to Math Standards?

Each Family Math Night station highlights a specific mathematics strand of the curriculum. The math connections given for each activity align with the *Principles and Standards for School Mathematics* (NCTM, 2000). One of the unique features of this book is the border around each activity page. There are five distinct borders that correlate with the five math content strands. The strands are number and operations; algebra; geometry; measurement; and data analysis and probability.

Number and Operations

Number and operations is a strand of the curriculum that promotes the understanding of numbers; number relationships; and the operations of addition, subtraction, multiplication, and division. The focus is on helping students develop number sense and computational proficiency.

Algebra

Algebra is a strand of the curriculum that highlights patterns, relationships, equality, functions, and models of representing math situations. The focus is on helping students recognize mathematical relationships, solve for unknowns, and establish ways of understanding and representing mathematics.

Geometry

Geometry is a strand of the curriculum that emphasizes the characteristics and properties of shape, spatial relationships, and visual representations. The focus is on encouraging students to utilize and strengthen skills in visualization, spatial reasoning, and geometric representations.

Measurement

Measurement is a strand of the curriculum that underscores the importance of understanding how objects are measured. Considering and experiencing appropriate units, processes, and tools are essential aspects of learning measurement.

Data Analysis and Probability

Data analysis and probability is the strand of the curriculum that highlights statistical information and the concepts associated with the likelihood of outcomes. It is important for students to understand how to collect, organize, analyze, and interpret data and to understand fundamental concepts of probability.

The Family Math Night stations are also connected to the NCTM (2000) process standards. These standards include problem solving, reasoning and proof, communication, connections, and representations. Problem solving is present in many of the activities as students and parents work together to reach solutions using knowledge and experience in mathematics. Reasoning and proof are associated with providing evidence of mathematical conjectures. As students explain and justify processes and answers, they are offering the reasoning and proof associated with sound mathematics. Communication is emphasized in the activities as students discuss and record their mathematical ideas and thinking processes. Connections are established as students come to understand how math ideas are related to each other and to the real world. Representations are given emphasis in the ways in which students model, organize, discuss, and record the mathematics associated with each activity.

Why Should We Use Manipulatives in Mathematics?

Using manipulatives in mathematics allows students to experience abstract concepts in a concrete manner. Building models to represent mathematical ideas and concepts strengthens the conceptual frameworks students construct as they apply math to everyday life. Manipulatives provide the means by which many students need to express the reasoning and evidence associated with the mathematical thinking. Using manipulatives to show how one derives an answer helps solidify understanding. Manipulatives offer students the tools to solve mathematical problems. Additionally, manipulatives often serve as the springboard for mathematical communication as students explain and justify how they solve a problem and/or approach a solution.

To encourage the successful use of math manipulatives, educators should think about how the manipulatives are organized and how they are made available to students. For example, sets of manipulatives can be prepared and stored in plastic bags, baskets, or other containers. The listed manipulatives must be made available to students and parents at each Family Math Night station.

Why is "Questions Parents Can Ask" Included?

Asking questions invites students to engage in mathematical communication. Questions promote mathematical thinking and encourage math discourse. We do not want the Family Math Night room to be a "quiet zone." Instead, we want to strive for a room full of active mathematics participants who are engaged in productive mathematics conversation. By promoting math discourse at Family Math Night, we will better prepare our students for the mathematical challenges ahead. Our role is to provide students with opportunities to hear, use, and come to know the richness of math discourse.

Why is There a Challenge for Each Activity?

Purposeful challenge serves to inspire and enlighten many students. Each Family Math Night activity includes a challenge that provides a possible extension of the activity. Sometimes students are so engaged in the activity that they want to investigate it further. Other times students go directly to the challenge as a way to increase the level of difficulty. Essentially, the challenges offer a way to differentiate the learning opportunities for students and their families.

What are Some Additional Tips for a Successful Family Math Night?

If you want high attendance at your Family Math Night, you need to advertise to students and their parents. Send home notices about the event (a sample notice to parents is found on page 80). Include the event in newsletters and on the school calendar. If possible provide food at the event. Offer incentives for students and parents. Some schools offer recognition to the class with the highest attendance. Other schools encourage students to attend by allowing participation in Family Math Night to serve as the night's homework or serve as extra credit. The possibilities are seemingly endless!

To accommodate many families you will need a large room or several large rooms. Position the tables and chairs in a manner that allows for maximum movement and comfort. Posting multiple copies of the directions and providing several sets of the materials allow you to have more than one family at each Family Math Night station. If younger siblings are invited, you may want to consider using some of the activities from the elementary-level version of this book titled *Family Math Night: Math Standards in Action*.

Providing a check-in table is a good idea. Parents and students can sign in or teachers can check off students on class lists. The check-in area is a place where students can obtain pencils and Family Math Night journals. The journals can be simple booklets of blank pages for students to record information related to the activities. A sample Family Math Night journal cover is found on page 81. Evaluation forms can also be distributed at the check-in area. A sample Family Math Night evaluation form is found on page 82. The information gathered from the evaluations will help you plan subsequent Family Math Nights.

What is the Teacher's Role During Family Math Night?

During Family Math Night, educators should facilitate the mathematical endeavors of students and parents. While visiting families at each station, educators should also encourage math dialogue and math thinking. Some of the consumable materials may need to be replenished, and some of the stations need to be monitored. However, be sure to take at least one moment during Family Math Night to notice how the event mathematically inspires and empowers students and parents!

Chapter Two:
Number and Operations

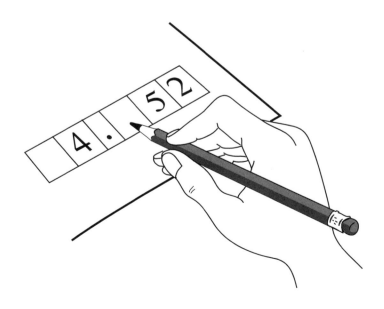

The Baseball Card Collection

Materials:

Pretend money (hundred dollar bills) or
  Base ten blocks (hundred flats) or
  Digi-blocks (hundred blocks)
Baseball cards (or index cards to represent
  the collection)

Helpful Hints:

Keeping track of how much money Marvin and Leon
spend and earn helps participants accurately solve
this problem.

Answers:

Marvin made $200.00
Leon lost $200.00

Challenge Answers:

Marvin made $500.00
Leon lost $500.00

Connections to Math Standards:

The Baseball Card Collection is an activity that
encourages students to think about the meaning
and effects of operations. Students are applying
mathematics to the real world as they find and
explain the solution.

The Baseball Card Collection

Math Question: How much money, if any, does Marvin or Leon make or lose?

Directions:

1. To role-play this math situation, decide who will be Marvin and who will be Leon.

2. Gather supplies to represent money and the baseball card collection. Role-play the math situation.

> *Marvin bought a baseball card collection from Leon for $300. Later, Marvin sold the baseball card collection back to Leon for $400. Marvin bought back the baseball card collection from Leon for $500. Again, Marvin sold the baseball card collection to Leon for $600. Overall, how much money, if any, did Marvin make or lose and how much money, if any, did Leon make or lose?*

3. Construct a table or chart that shows how you solved this problem.

Questions Parents Can Ask:

How can you keep track of the money?

How could you use negative numbers in this problem?

Does it matter how much money Marvin or Leon has in the beginning? Why or why not?

Challenge:

If the pattern continues, how much money, if any, will Marvin make or lose after he buys back *and* sells for the fifth time? What about Leon?

How Low Can You Go?

Materials:

Place value frames (see page 83)
Number cubes (dice)
Place value names reference chart (see page 84)
Overhead markers and wipes (optional)

Helpful Hints:

Provide multiple copies of the place value frames.

If place value frames are mounted and laminated, players can use overhead markers to write on them and then erase the frames for multiple uses.

The place value names reference chart helps participants read the number correctly.

Answers:

Answers will vary.

Connections to Math Standards:

How Low Can You Go? is an activity that encourages students to work with number relationships by comparing and ordering decimals.

How Low Can You Go?

*Math Question: Which decimal fraction is smaller?
How do you know?*

Directions:

1. Each player uses her/his own place value frame.

2. Roll a number cube and write the number that comes up in one of your five sections. The other player also writes the same number in one of her/his five sections (not necessarily the same section because each player may use a different strategy to choose which section).

3. Continue taking turns rolling the number cube and writing the decimal digits until all of the sections are filled.

4. Compare the numbers created. The player with the smallest number wins the round. Remember to accurately read the number. For example, 34.152 is thirty-four and one hundred fifty-two thousandths. The word "and" is only used at the decimal point. To encourage math language and thinking about decimal values, *avoid* reading the number as "34 point 152."

5. Play three rounds.

Questions Parents Can Ask:

Which decimal place is that? How do you know?

Why did you place the digit there? What was your strategy?

Challenge:

Try playing to get the largest number.

Digits in a Row

Materials:

    Calculators

    Number tiles (digits 1 through 9)

Helpful Hints:

The number tiles help participants keep the digits in consecutive order. If number tiles are not available you can make them out of paper (see page 85). Highlight the fact that there are several correct answers to this math problem.

Answers: Other solutions are possible.

$$1 + 2 + 34 - 5 + 67 - 8 + 9$$
$$12 + 3 - 4 + 5 + 67 + 8 + 9$$
$$123 + 4 - 5 + 67 - 89$$
$$123 + 45 - 67 + 8 - 9$$
$$123 - 4 - 5 - 6 - 7 + 8 - 9$$
$$123 - 45 - 67 + 89$$

Challenge Answers: Other solutions are possible.

$$98 - 76 + 54 + 3 + 21$$
$$9 + 8 + 76 + 5 + 4 - 3 + 2 - 1$$
$$98 - 7 - 6 + 5 + 4 + 3 + 2 + 1$$
$$98 - 7 + 6 - 5 + 4 + 3 + 2 - 1$$

Connections to Math Standards:

Digits in a Row is an activity that helps students gain further experiences with the meaning and effects of arithmetic operations.

Digits in a Row

Math Question: How can you add and/or subtract combinations of the digits to equal 100?

Directions:

1. **Line up the number tiles in consecutive order.**

   1   2   3   4   5   6   7   8   9

2. **Add and/or subtract the digits in consecutive order to form an expression equal to 100.**

3. **Single digits can be used or digits can be pushed together to form two-place or three-place numbers. For example, the first number can be 1 or 12 or 123. Try to find more than one correct solution.**

Note: Digits must be in consecutive order and may only be used once for each expression.

Questions Parents Can Ask:

Which operation will help you get closer to 100?

How can you keep track of the equations you have already tried?

What will happen if you start with a negative number?

Challenge:

Try placing the digits in descending order (9-1) to form an expression equal to 100.

Salary Selections

Materials:

Calculators
Salary option cards (see page 86)
Scissors

Helpful Hints:

The salary option cards are designed with a work space for students to use to complete calculations. Recording all calculations on these cards allows participants to readily compare each of the pay options. Have many copies of the salary option cards available for students.

Answers:

Option D offers the best pay for a six-hour day. Option A is the best choice for an eight-hour day. The chart below provides the totals for each pay option.

Pay Periods	Pay Option A	Pay Option B	Pay Option C	Pay Option D
Six-Hour Day	$63.00	$72.00	$75.00	$90.00 per day
Eight-Hour Day	$255.00	$96.00	$75.00	$90.00 per day

Challenge Answers:

Weekly Pay	$1,275.00	$480.00	$375.00	$450.00
Monthly Pay (Weekly Pay x 4)	$5,100.00	$1,920.00	$1,500.00	$1,800.00
Yearly Pay (Weekly Pay x 52)	$66,300.00	$24,960.00	$19,500.00	$23,400.00

Connections to Math Standards:

Salary Selections is an activity requiring students to complete multiple operations in order to determine the best pay option. The activity enables students to understand the meaning of arithmetic operations and the comparison of the effects of such operations when solving problems.

Salary Selections

Math Question: Which salary option is the best?

A newly hired video store manager must choose from the offered salary options. Work as a family to determine the best choice based on a five-day workweek.

Directions:

1. Cut out the four salary option cards. Shuffle and distribute cards to family members.

2. Predict and record in your math journal which option would be most lucrative for an employee working a six-hour day. Verify your prediction by displaying your calculations in a table. You may write on the cards.

3. Determine if the same pay option is still the best if a video store manager works an eight-hour day.

Questions Parents Can Ask:

*Was your prediction the best salary option?

*How does the length of the workday affect the best salary choice?

*What is the difference in the daily salary between the highest paying option and the lowest paying option?

Challenge:

Calculate the monthly salary (based on four weeks per month) and the annual salary (based on 52 weeks per year) for each pay option for an eight-hour workday.

Fraction Designs

Materials:

Pattern blocks
Calculators
Scissors and paper

Helpful Hints:

Provide paper and scissors for students who may choose to trace and cut some of the pattern block shapes to determine the value.

Answers:

Yellow Hexagon $3/4$
Red Trapezoid $1/2$ of $3/4 = 3/8$
Blue Rhombus $1/3$ of $3/4 = 1/4$
Green Triangle $1/6$ of $3/4 = 1/8$
Designs with a value of $4^{3/4}$ will vary.
One correct solution is a design including three hexagons, two trapezoids, six rhombuses, and two triangles.

Challenge Answers:

Percentage is value of green divided by total value ($4^{3/4}$ or 4.75) times 100. If only one green triangle is used the answer is 2.63%. For additional green triangles multiply 2.63% times the number of green triangles used.

$$\frac{1/8}{4^{3/4}} = \frac{0.125}{4.75} \approx 0.0263 = 2.63\%$$

Connections to Math Standards:

Fraction Designs requires flexible thinking in computing with rational numbers. The use of pattern blocks provides a connection to geometry and measurement concepts and utilizes concrete materials in the process of determining the fractional values.

Fraction Designs

Math Question: What is the value of the pattern blocks if the yellow hexagon equals 3/4?

Directions:

1. Assign the value of 3/4 to the yellow hexagon.

2. Determine the value of the red trapezoid, blue rhombus, and green triangle based on the value of the yellow hexagon.

3. Create a design with a value of 4 3/4, including at least one green triangle.

Questions Parents Can Ask:

*How did you determine the value of each block?

*How many green triangles does it take to make a yellow hexagon?

*What is the greatest number of blocks that could be used to build the design? What is the least number of blocks?

Challenge:

Calculate the percentage of the design that is green.

Establishing Order

Materials:

Sequence cards A-I (see page 87)
Blank sequence cards (see page 88)
Calculators

Helpful Hints:

Provide several sets of the sequence cards.
Copy sets of the sequence cards on different colored paper to help keep the sets organized (card stock works nicely). Fold each card along the dotted line to create a standing tent. Provide several blank sequence cards for the challenge.

Answers:

The sequence from smallest value to largest value is
I G F H B D C E A

Connections to Math Standards:

Establishing Order allows students to use estimation and number sense to sequence the cards from the smallest value to the largest value, and then verify the sequence using their computation skills.

Establishing Order

Math Question: What is the value for each card?

Directions:

1. Read each sequence card and estimate the value. Write estimates in your math journal.

2. Place the cards in order from least to greatest based on your estimates.

3. Verify your sequence by calculating the answer for each sequence card.

4. Adjust your sequence as necessary.

Questions Parents Can Ask:

What strategy did you use to find your estimate?

How did your estimated sequence compare to the actual sequence?

What is the advantage of estimating before calculating?

Challenge:

Create a new sequence card and determine where it belongs in the sequence.

Chapter Three:
Algebra

Spiders and Ants

Birds Migrating to Florida

Box Dilemma

ABCs and 123s

Pascal's Patterns

Produce Equations

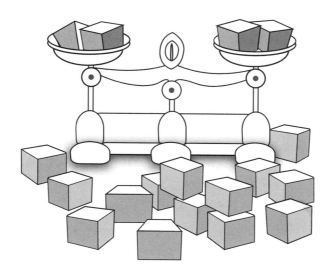

Spiders and Ants

Materials:

Colored pencils
Counters (translucent chips)
Spiders and ants spinner (see page 89)
Number chart (see page 90)
Paper clips

Helpful Hints:

To use the spinner, place the paper clip in the center of the spinner. Place pencil point through the paper clip at the center of the spinner. Holding the pencil securely with one hand, spin the paper clip with the other hand. If students are unfamiliar with this process, you may need to demonstrate how to use the spinner.

Have many copies of the number chart available.

Answers:

There are several different correct answers:
0 spiders and 16 ants
3 spiders and 12 ants
6 spiders and 8 ants
9 spiders and 4 ants
12 spiders and 0 ants

Connections to Math Standards:

Spiders and Ants is an activity that presents an algebraic thinking situation that encourages students to model and solve contextual problems through representations.

Spiders and Ants

Math Question: How many spiders and how many ants are in the bug jar full of 96 legs?

Directions:

1. **Ants have six legs. Spiders have eight legs. The object of the game is to be the player who spins the quantity that allows her/ him to have *exactly* 96 total legs in the shared bug jar. Begin with an empty bug jar.**

2. **Take turns spinning the spinner and discussing the results. If your early spins land on "subtract," use negative numbers.**

   Note: Subtracting a spider means subtracting eight legs. Subtracting an ant means subtracting six legs.

3. **Draw a diagram, make a list, or use a model to keep a running total of the number of legs in the bug jar. Option: You can color and/or place counters on the number chart to keep a total of the legs in the bug jar. Discuss strategies for winning the game.**

Questions Parents Can Ask:

How can you keep track of the number of legs in the bug jar?

Where do you want the spinner to land next? Why?

Are there several ways to get to 96 legs? How do you know?

Challenge:

What if there were more legs in the jar?

Birds Migrating to Florida

Materials:

Snap cubes or multilink cubes
Graph paper

Helpful Hints:

To predict the number of birds on any given day in this pattern, students need to think about the relationship between the given day number and given number of birds.

Answers:

28 birds will be in Town Square on the tenth day.
43 birds will be in Town Square on the fifteenth day.

Challenge Answer:

To obtain the number of birds on any given day, we need to multiply the number of days (n) by 3 and subtract 2.
$3n - 2$

Connections to Math Standards:

Birds Migrating to Florida is an activity that presents an algebra problem that encourages students to notice patterns and represent problem situations through diagrams, lists, and models. Students organize and analyze information to find and explain the solution.

Birds Migrating to Florida

Math Question: Using the given pattern, how many birds will be in Town Square on the tenth day?

Directions:

1. Use snap cubes and/or graph paper to construct a model or create a table to find the answer.

> *Birds are migrating to Town Square in Fort Lauderdale, Florida. On the first day one bird is in Town Square. On the second day four birds are in Town Square. On the third day seven birds are in Town Square. On the fourth day ten birds are in Town Square. At this rate, how many birds will be in Town Square in Fort Lauderdale on the tenth day?*

2. Use the information that you know to find out how many birds will be in Town Square on the tenth day.

Questions Parents Can Ask:

*What pattern(s) do you see?

*What is the relationship between the day and the number of birds?

*At this rate, how many birds will be in Town Square on day fifteen?

Challenge:

Write an expression that describes the nth term.

Box Dilemma

Materials:

Stationary scales or model scales
18 cubes (to represent boxes)

Helpful Hints:

Using a real scale or balance can actually serve to confuse the problem because the heavier box is hypothetical. Use a stationary scale or a scale without the base as a prop to help this problem-solving situation.

Answer: One possible solution involves the following steps:

1. First use of the scale: six boxes in one pan, 6 boxes in the other pan, and six boxes out. If the scale is balanced, you know it is one of the six out. If one side of the scale is heavier, you know it is one of the six. In either case, you have narrowed down the possibilities to six.
2. Second use of the scale: two boxes in one pan, two boxes in the other pan, and two boxes out. If the scale is balanced, you know it is one of the two out. If one side of the scale is heavier, you know it is one of the two. In either case, you have narrowed down the possibilities to two.
3. Third use of the scale: one box in one pan, one box in the other pan, and one box out. If the scale is balanced, you know it is the one that is out. If one side of the scale is heavier, you know which box is heavier. In either case, you found the heaviest box.

Challenge Answer: 2

Connections to Math Standards:

Box Dilemma presents an algebra problem that helps participants model and solve contextual problems using various representations.

Box Dilemma

Math Question: How can you find the heaviest box using the pan balance only three times?

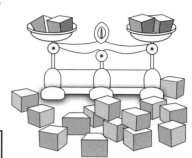

Directions:

1. Use cubes and the stationary scale to find the solution to the following math situation.

> *There are 18 boxes. All the boxes look the same, but one weighs more than the others. How can you find out which box weighs more if you can only use the pan balance scale three times?*

2. Think about putting more than one cube at a time in each pan of the balance.

Questions Parents Can Ask:

What did you find out with the first use of the scale?

How many boxes did you eliminate?

How can you eliminate more than one box at a time?

Challenge:

What is the minimum number of times the pan balance is needed if there are nine boxes?

ABCs and 123s

Materials:

    Sets of transparent number tiles (digits 0-9)
    Equation strips (see page 91)
    Scissors
    Index cards

Helpful Hints:

Transparent number tiles are ideal for this activity because they allow students to arrange and rearrange the tiles as unknowns are solved. Additionally, students can still see the variable through the number tile. Six sets of 0-9 tiles should be available for each family because the variables are represented multiple times on the equation strips. If number tiles are not available, students can record equations and answers in their math journals.

Answers:

A = 5	F = 0
B = 2	G = 1
C = 9	H = 3
D = 7	I = 4
E = 8	J = 6

Connections to Math Standards:

ABCs and 123s encourages students to think algebraically as they solve for variables based upon the properties and relationships of the numerals used in various algebraic equations.

ABCs and 123s

Math Question: What is the value of each variable?

<u>Directions:</u>

1. **Cut out the eight equation strips. Each variable (letter) represents a unique number 0-9.**
2. **Examine the strips and arrange them in a way that helps you solve the equations.**
3. **Use the number tiles to identify the value of each variable.**

<u>Questions Parents Can Ask:</u>

****Which equations did you start with and why?***

****Could any of the equations be eliminated because you already know the values?***

****How did the final sequence you used to solve the equations compare to your original sequence?***

****Could there be more than one set of values for the variables?***

<u>Challenge:</u>

Use index cards to create your own set of equations for which each variable has only one possible value.

Pascal's Patterns

Materials:

Pascal's Triangle (see page 92)
Colored pencils
Calculators

Helpful Hints:

Provide several copies of Pascal's Triangle.
Participants may explore several numerical and/or
visual patterns, which may require a new copy of
the triangular array for each exploration.

Answers:

```
                    1
                  1   1
                1   2   1
              1   3   3   1
            1   4   6   4   1
          1   5  10  10   5   1
        1   6  15  20  15   6   1
      1   7  21  35  35  21   7   1
    1   8  28  56  70  56  28   8   1
  1   9  36  84 126 126  84  36   9   1
1  10  45 120 210 252 210 120  45  10   1
1  11  55 165 330 462 462 330 165  55  11   1
```

**Identified patterns will vary and may be found in rows
and/or along diagonals. Some examples include 0th diagonals are all ones, 1st diagonals increase by one, and
numbers repeat in each row from the center outward.**

Challenge Answer: The sum of row 100 is 2^{100}.

Connections to Math Standards:

Pascal's Patterns is based on a triangular array of
numbers known as Pascal's Triangle (credited to Blaise
Pascal). While the triangle was created to display the
number of ways in which a particular event can happen, multiple number and visual patterns also exist.

Pascal's Patterns

Math Question: How many patterns can you find in Pascal's Triangle?

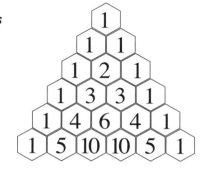

Directions:

1. Take a copy of Pascal's Triangle and examine the array of numerals. Try to find patterns in the rows and diagonals.

2. Complete at least the next six rows of numbers based on the patterns.

3. Record at least five different patterns that exist within the array of numbers. For example, there is a diagonal row of triangular numbers including 1, 3, 6, 10, 15, . . .

4. Choose a number between 1 and 10, and color in all of the multiples of that particular number.

5. Complete another triangle, and color the multiples of a different number. Compare the two Pascal's Triangle patterns.

Questions Parents Can Ask:

What do you notice about the sums of each row?

What is the estimated percentage of shaded numbers in your shaded triangles? How do you know?

How many lines of symmetry are in your triangular pattern?

Challenge:

Try to determine the sum for row 100.

$x = y +$ ☁

$x = y +$ ☁

$x = y +$ ☁

$x = y +$ ☁

$x = y +$ ☁

$x = y +$ ☁

$x = y +$ ☁

$x = y +$ ☁

$x = y +$ ☁

$x = y +$ ☁

$x = y +$ ☁

Produce Equations

Materials:

Snap cubes (yellow, orange, and red)

Helpful Hints:

The snap cubes enable participants to simulate substitution. The specific colors represent the three fruit types.

Answers:

One grapefruit and two apples do *not* equal three pears.

given	$3p = 4a$
given	$1g = 2a + 1p$
what you are looking for	$1g + 2a \stackrel{?}{=} 3p$
substitute	$2a + 1p$ for $1g$
from second given equation	$2a + 1p + 2a \stackrel{?}{=} 3p$
combine $2a + 2a$	$4a + 1p \stackrel{?}{=} 3p$
substitute	$3p$ for $4a$
from first given equation	$3p + 1p \stackrel{?}{=} 3p$
combine $3p + 1p$	$4p \neq 3p$

One way to rewrite the quantities to make them equal:
One grapefruit + two apples − one pear = three pears

Connections to Math Standards:

Produce Equations is an activity that encourages students to use symbolic algebra to represent situations and solve problems.

Produce Equations

Math Question: Are the given quantities equal?

If three pears weigh the same as four apples
and
*One grapefruit weighs the same as
two apples and one pear,*
will
*One grapefruit and two apples weigh
the same as three pears?*

Directions:

1. **Read the question above and use the snap cubes to model the problem.**

2. **Decide whether the equation "one grapefruit and two apples weigh the same as three pears" is true.**

3. **If you think the equation is true, explain why. If you think the equation is not true, rewrite it to make it true.**

Questions Parents Can Ask:

How might the snap cubes help to solve this problem?

How do the fruit values compare to one another? How do you know?

Challenge:

Write additional equations using apples, pears, and grapefruit in your math journal.

Chapter Four:
Geometry

All Squared Up

Party with Pentominoes

Line Up the Attribute Blocks

Nets Under Construction

Newspaper Networks

Pythagorean Triples

All Squared Up

Materials:

Colored pencils or crayons
Square grid paper (see page 93)

Helpful Hints:

Have many copies of the square grid paper available.

Answer:

30 squares, including:
One 4 x 4
Four 3 x 3
Nine 2 x 2
Sixteen 1 x 1

Formula for the sum of all squares in a square of size n _x_ n.
$1^2 + 2^2 + 3^2 + \ldots + n^2$

Challenge Answer:

55 squares, including:
One 5 x 5
Four 4 x 4
Nine 3 x 3
Sixteen 2 x 2
Twenty-five 1 x 1

Connections to Math Standards:

All Squared Up is an activity that encourages students to analyze characteristics and properties of two-dimensional geometric shapes—specifically, squares.

All Squared Up

Math Question: How many squares do you see in the 4 x 4 figure?

Directions:

1. Look at the 4 x 4 figure. How many squares do you see?

2. Draw the 4 x 4 figure on the square grid paper. Use colored pencils or crayons to mark squares as you count them.

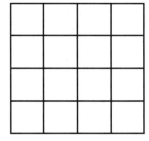

3. List how many squares there are of each size. Organize the information and look for patterns.

Questions Parents Can Ask:

How many squares do you see? Are all the squares the same size?

How could you describe the size of the squares you have already counted?

Which squares are the smallest?

Challenge:

Use the square grid paper to draw a new figure that is 5 x 5. How many squares do you see?

Party with Pentominoes

Materials:

Square tiles
Graph paper
Scissors
Answer key (see page 94)
Folder or envelope

Helpful Hints:

Display at least one of the pentominoes as an example.

Place the answer key in a folder or envelope labeled "Answers" so that participants try creating several different pentominoes before looking at answers.

Answers:

See answer key (see page 94)

Connections to Math Standards:

Party with Pentominoes is an activity that helps students develop richer understandings of how to apply transformations and symmetry to analyze geometrical situations. Students explore various positions and orientations of shapes.

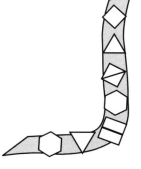

Party with Pentominoes

Math Questions: How can the squares be arranged to make 12 different pentominoes? How can the pentominoes be arranged to form a rectangle?

Directions:

1. Make a pentomino by grouping five squares together so that every square has at least one of its sides in common with at least one other square.

2. One example of a pentomino is a rectangle formed by lining up all five squares. Try making more complex pentominoes (such as a "T" form). There are 12 different pentominoes.

   Note: If the pentominoes are congruent (same shape flipped or rotated), they are not considered different.

3. Draw your pentominoes on graph paper and cut them out.

4. Try using all 12 pentominoes to construct a 6 x 10 rectangle.

Questions Parents Can Ask:

How do you know that you have made a different pentomino?

Do all of the pentominoes have the same area? Do all of the pentominoes have the same perimeter?

Which pentominoes can be folded to make a cube without a lid?

Challenge:

Try using all 12 pentominoes to construct a 5 x 12 rectangle or a 4 x 15 rectangle or a 3 x 20 rectangle.

Line Up the Attribute Blocks

Materials:

Sets of attribute blocks

Helpful Hints:

A complete set of attribute blocks includes only one block of each shape, size, color, and thickness (60 blocks). Help participants keep sets separate by providing bags or containers.

Answers:

Answers will vary.
One possible "lineup" may begin with a large, red, thick triangle. Next could be a *small*, red, thick triangle or a large, *blue*, thick triangle or a large, red, *thin* triangle or a large, red, thick *rectangle*.

Connections to Math Standards:

Line Up the Attribute Blocks is an activity that provides students with further opportunities to analyze characteristics and properties of geometric shapes and to use problem-solving strategies.

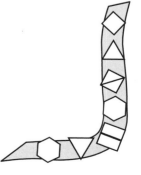

Line Up the Attribute Blocks

Math Question: How is each attribute block different from another attribute block?

Directions:

1. Each participant chooses 15 attribute blocks from the set.

2. The first person sets one block on the table. The next person chooses which block to "line up" next. The block must be different from the previous block in *only one way* (shape, size, color, or thickness).

3. Participants take turns lining up blocks that are different from the previous block in *only one way*. Blocks may also be placed between other blocks or before the first block, as long as each block is different in *only one way*.

4. If you do not have any blocks that can be played next, you may choose to "trade" one of your blocks for any block left in the set. Each participant is allowed three "trades" per game. If you do not have a block to play and do not have any "trades" left, you must skip your turn. The winner is the first person to place all 15 blocks.

Questions Parents Can Ask:

How is this block different from the previous block?

Which attributes do the blocks have in common?

What is your strategy for using all of your blocks?

Challenge:

Try using the entire set of attribute blocks or try changing the line into a circle.

Nets Under Construction

Materials:

> Geometric solids
> Tag board
> Scissors
> Rulers
> Compass
> Clear tape

Helpful Hints:

> The geometric solids provided should include, but not be limited to, cylinders, triangular pyramids, rectangular pyramids, triangular prisms, rectangular prisms (including cubes), and cones.

Answers:

> Solutions will vary based on the choice of geometric solids. The task is self-correcting because students may compare the two solids for congruency.

Connections to Math Standards:

> *Nets Under Construction* provides students with the opportunity to identify and describe geometric solids. In order to build the solids, students must first identify the shapes that make up the faces, bases, and surfaces of the solid. Students must create congruent shapes in the correct arrangement and then fold to form the new solid.

Nets Under Construction

Math Question: What does the 2-D net look like for a 3-D figure?

Directions:

1. **Choose from the collection of geometric solids.**

2. **Draw a net on tag board for the solid using the actual solid as a measurement and tracing tool.**

   Example:

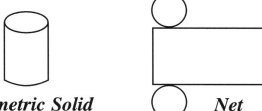

   Geometric Solid   *Net*

3. **Cut out the tracing to create the net.**

4. **Fold and assemble the net to create a solid congruent to the original.**

Questions Parents Can Ask:

*What are the shapes of the face, bases, and/or surfaces of the solid?

*How did you determine the arrangement of the shapes to form the net?

*Could a different net be created and folded to create the same solid?

Challenge:

Try making several noncongruent nets, which can be folded to form the same size cube.

Newspaper Networks

Materials:

Newspaper networks map (see page 95)
Counters or bingo chips (30 per set)
Colored pencils
Rulers

Helpful Hints:

The counters help students keep track of their paths
and serve as indicators of where they have already
traveled. Students may prefer to use colored pencils to
mark the paths. Provide many copies of the newspaper
networks map.

Answers:

There is more than one possible path without passing
any house more than once.

Challenge Answers:

Answers will vary, but should include the paths that
connect the homes.

Connections to Math Standards:

Newspaper Networks enables students to enhance
their skills of visualization and reasoning about spatial
relationships. Concern with efficiency is one of the
applications of networks in mathematics.

Newspaper Networks

Math Question: What is an efficient way to deliver the newspapers throughout the neighborhood?

Directions:

1. Look at the newspaper networks map.

2. Find an efficient path to deliver newspapers to every home without visiting a single home more than once.

3. Use the counters or colored pencils to monitor the homes already passed and to keep track of the path.

Questions Parents Can Ask:

Where will you go next?

Is there more than one efficient path to follow to deliver the papers?

How many different paths can you find?

Challenge:

Design your own newspaper networks map in your math journal.

Pythagorean Triples

Materials:

Centimeter grid paper

Centimeter cubes

Helpful Hints:

The grid paper and cubes provide a hands-on approach for representing $a^2 + b^2 = c^2$.

Answers:

Pythagorean Triples:

3, 4, **5**

5, 12, **13**

6, 8, **10**

8, 15, **17**

12, 16, **20**

Challenge Answers:

7, 24, **25**

Connections to Math Standards:

Pythagorean Triples is a geometry task in which students draw right triangles and create a visual model of the Pythagorean theorem, $a^2 + b^2 = c^2$.

Pythagorean Triples

Math Question: What is the third value in the Pythagorean triples?

Directions:

1. **Draw a right angle on the grid paper with one side 3 cm and the other side 4 cm long.** *(see figure to right.)*

2. **Sketch the square for each of the two sides.**

3. **Draw the hypotenuse (diagonal) to form a triangle.**

4. **Using a 5 x 5 array of centimeter cubes, create the square for the hypotenuse. Place this array on the hypotenuse and compare the area of the hypotenuse square with the sum of the areas of the squares of the legs.**

5. **Complete the following Pythagorean triples:**
   5, 12, ?   6, 8, ?   8, 15, ?   12, 16, ?

Questions Parents Can Ask:

   **What relationship do you notice among the areas of the squares?*

   **How many Pythagorean triples do you think there are? Why?*

Challenge:

   Find the missing lengths in this Pythagorean triple ____, 24, ____.

Chapter Five: Measurement

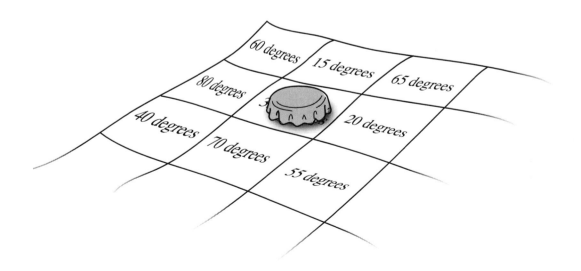

Big Bubbles

Materials:

Bubble solution
Straws
String
Scissors
Plastic rulers
Paper towels
Calculators

Helpful Hints:

Add glycerin to the bubble solution to make stronger bubbles.

When rulers are coated in bubble solution, they can slide into the bubble for measuring.

Have plenty of paper towels to clean up bubble solution.

Answers:

Bubble measurements will vary. Bubbles on the table form a hemisphere (half of a sphere).
The distance around a circle is called circumference. For all circles, the ratio of the circumference to the diameter is always the same. The ratio is called π (pi). The value for π is approximately 3.14 or ²²/₇.

The formula for circumference is C = πd or C = 2πr

Connections to Math Standards:

Big Bubbles **is an activity that encourages students to develop and use strategies to determine the diameter and circumference of circles.**

Big Bubbles

Math Question: What is the relationship between diameter and circumference?

Directions:

1. Dip one end of the straw into the bubble solution. Cover the top of the straw and transport some of the bubble solution to the bubble-blowing surface (table).

2. Gently blow into the straw. Have your partner coat a ruler with bubble solution and slide the ruler into the bubble to measure the diameter.

3. When the bubble bursts, use the ring left on the surface to measure the diameter of the bubble. To find the circumference, lay string on the ring of the bubble and then measure the string using a ruler.

4. Blow five bubbles. Record the diameters (d) and circumferences (c) of the bubbles in your math journal. Use a calculator to solve c ÷ d for each bubble. Discuss the ratio of the circumference to the diameter (pi).

Questions Parents Can Ask:

How much bigger is the circumference than the diameter?

What is the radius of the bubble ring (half of the diameter)?

What shape does the bubble form?

Challenge:

Try blowing bubbles inside of bubbles and measuring the diameters and circumferences.

Try Angles

Materials:

Angle mats (see page 96)
Bottle caps or counters
Protractors

Helpful Hints:

Participants may need help using the protractor.

Answers:

All triangles have three angles. The sum of the measures of these angles equals 180 degrees. Equilateral triangles have equal angles (and equal sides).

Connections to Math Standards:

Try Angles is an activity that allows students to understand, select, and use angle measurements to form triangles.

Try Angles

Math Question: Which angles form a triangle?

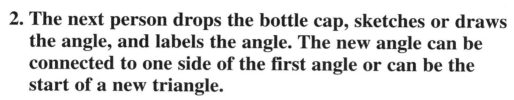

Directions:

1. Drop the bottle cap on the angle mat to determine which angle you will draw. Sketch the angle or use a protractor to draw the angle in your math journal. Label the angle in degrees.

2. The next person drops the bottle cap, sketches or draws the angle, and labels the angle. The new angle can be connected to one side of the first angle or can be the start of a new triangle.

3. Players continue taking turns dropping the bottle cap, sketching or drawing angles, and labeling angles. Each new angle can be connected to previous angles or can be the start of a new triangle.

4. When a player adds the third angle to form a triangle, s/he earns 100 points.

   Note: All triangles have three angles. The sum of the measures of these angles equals 180 degrees.

5. The game ends after 18 angles have been drawn.

Questions Parents Can Ask:

Which angle do you need to complete a triangle? How do you know?

Which type of triangle has equal angles?

Challenge:

Try making other triangles with the protractor.

Mystery Figure

Materials:

    Graph paper
    Rulers
    Calculators

Helpful Hints:

You can start at either bottom corner. There is more than one solution.

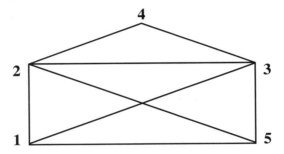

Answers:

Other solutions are possible.
    1, 2, 3, 4, 2, 5, 3, 1, 5 or
    5, 3, 2, 4, 3, 1, 2, 5, 1

Answers will vary, but should be in square units.
    For the rectangle, A = *lw*
    For the triangle, A = $\frac{1}{2}$ *bh*

Connections to Math Standards:

Mystery Figure is an activity that encourages participants to use appropriate measurement techniques and formulas to determine the area of rectangles and triangles.

Mystery Figure

Math Questions: How can you draw the figure without lifting your pencil? How can the area of the figure be determined?

Directions:

1. Draw the figure on graph paper without lifting your pencil and without retracing any of the line segments.

Note: You can cross a line segment or go through a point more than one time.

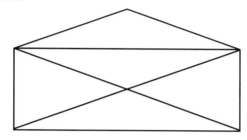

2. Here's a hint: Start at a bottom corner. The first line is vertical. There is more than one solution.

3. Find the total area (in square units) of the figure.

Questions Parents Can Ask:

*How many line segments are in the figure?

*How can you find the area of the rectangle?

*What is the area of the figure? How do you know?

Challenge:

Try making a different mystery figure with the same area.

Triangular Teasers

Materials:

Geoboards

Geobands

Helpful Hints:

Students may choose to enclose a triangle within a rectangle with sides parallel to the geoboard. This strategy enables learners to subtract the unused areas of the rectangle to determine the area of the triangle.

Answers:

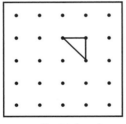

smallest triangle
area = $^1/_2$ square units

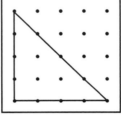

largest triangle
area = 8 square units

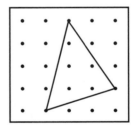

area = $5^1/_2$ square units

Challenge Answers:

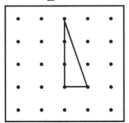

$1^1/_2$ square units

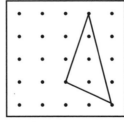

$3^1/_2$ square units

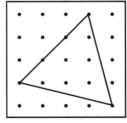

$7^1/_2$ square units

Connections to Math Standards:

Triangular Teasers provides a concrete representation for students to explore making large and small triangles. This task highlights the connection of measurement and geometry.

Triangular Teasers

Math Question: How do you determine the area of a triangle on a geoboard?

Directions:

1. Use the geoboard and geobands to create and name several shapes, such as triangles, quadrilaterals, and various other polygons.

2. Create a triangle with the smallest possible area. Create a triangle with the largest possible area.

3. Try to create a triangle with an area of $5\frac{1}{2}$ square units.

4. Use Pick's theorem to verify (and adjust, if needed) the area of your triangle.

Pick's Theorem

Area = B/2 + I – 1

B is the number of pegs along the borders of the shape;
I is the number of pegs in the interior of the shape

Questions Parents Can Ask:

Can you create noncongruent triangles with the same area?

What is another strategy you could use to find the area of the triangles?

Challenge:

Create triangles with the following areas:
$1\frac{1}{2}$ square units, $3\frac{1}{2}$ square units, $7\frac{1}{2}$ square units.

This Room on That Paper

Materials:

100-foot tape measures
Rulers
Drawing paper

Helpful Hints:

Provide several tape measures.

Answers:

Answers will vary based on the scale.

Connections to Math Standards:

This Room on That Paper allows students to create a scale model of the room. The task highlights the visual effects of scale drawings on the dimensions of a large room. These effects are present in the one-dimensional linear measures as well as the two-dimensional area of the room.

This Room on That Paper

Math Question: What scale could be used to draw this room on a sheet of paper?

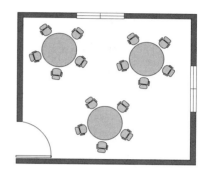

Directions:

1. Use the tape measure to measure and record the dimensions of this room.

2. Consider an appropriate scale which would enable a model of this room to be drawn on a sheet of paper.

3. Draw a scale model of this room.

4. Add windows and a few other items (door, tables, etc.) to your drawing.

Questions Parents Can Ask:

*What will be the length of the room on the scale model? Why?

*What effect does the scale factor have on area?

*When are scale models used in the real world?

Challenge:

Draw an enlarged version of your pencil. Label the scale.

Cookie Constructions

Materials:

> Rulers
> Compasses
> Scissors
> Inch grid paper
> Cookie construction cutouts (see page 97)
> Calculators

Helpful Hints:

> Students may choose to trace the cookie on the grid paper to estimate the area. Others may choose to cut the cookie into pieces to compare the area of other cookies. Provide several cookie cutouts.

Answers:

> Cookies cutouts will vary but should have an area of approximately 12 square inches. The actual area of a circle with a four-inch diameter is 12.57 square inches.
> > The area of a rectangle is l x w
> > The area of a triangle is $1/2$ b x h
> > The area of a trapezoid is $1/2$ $(b_1 + b_2)$ x h

Challenge Answer:

> To increase the area four times, double the radius.

Connections to Math Standards:

> *Cookie Constructions* is an activity that provides students with opportunities to explore the same area among different shapes and devise strategies for constructing such shapes.

Cookie Constructions

Math Question: Do the square, rectangle, trapezoid, and triangle have about the same area as the circle?

Directions:

1. **Cut out the cookies. Use a calculator to determine the area of the cookie.**
   Note: Area of a circle is π times r². Use 3.14 for pi.

2. **Draw several other different-shaped cookies with approximately the same area as the circular cookie. The new cookie shapes should include a rectangle, trapezoid, and triangle.**

3. **Determine the area of each new cookie to verify that the area is approximately the same as the original cookie.**

   The area of a rectangle is l x w
   The area of a triangle is $\frac{1}{2} b$ x h
   The area of a trapezoid is $\frac{1}{2} (b_1 + b_2)$ x h

Questions Parents Can Ask:

How could you prove the area is about the same?

What shapes do you see within the trapezoid?

What is another strategy you could use to find the area of a triangle?

Challenge:

Construct a circular cookie with an area four times that of the original cookie using a compass.

Chapter Six:
Data Analysis and Probability

Deep-Sea Diving

Lollipops in the Bag

Pendulum Swing Experiment

A Day in My Life

Chance for Freebies

Spinner Maker

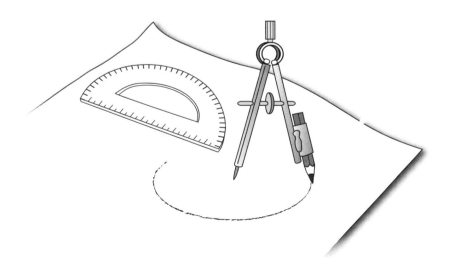

Deep-Sea Diving

Materials:

Bag of gems or cubes or other counters
Calculators
Mean, median, mode, and range definitions
(see page 98)

Helpful Hints:

Glass gems can often be purchased at the dollar store.

Post definitions of mean, median, mode, and range.

Answers:

An example set of data is provided; however, students' data sets will vary based on size of hand and size of gems.
12, 13, 14, 14, 14, 15, 15, 17, 18, 18
Mean = 15
Median = 14.5
Mode = 14
Range = 6
500 ÷ 15 = 33.33, which would require 34 dives
500 ÷ 14.5 = 34.48, which would require 35 dives
500 ÷ 14 = 35.71, which would require 36 dives

Connections to Math Standards:

Deep-Sea Diving is an activity that encourages students to collect data and to use appropriate statistical methods to analyze and interpret data.

Deep-Sea Diving

Math Question: How many handfuls will it take to retrieve 500 gems?

Directions:

1. Use the bag of gems (or cubes) to find the average amount that can be retrieved with one handful. Reach in the bag, get a handful, and then count the gems. Record the number of gems in the handful in your math journal. Place the gems back in the bag and repeat the process nine more times.

> *As a deep-sea diver, you just discovered a treasure chest that is firmly attached to the ocean floor. The gems can be removed, but only one handful at a time. You have ten practice dives to find out how many dives it will take you to recover 500 gems.*

2. Record the number of gems retrieved in each of the ten handfuls. Find the mean, median, mode, and range of the set of data that you collected. Using this information, discuss how many dives are needed to retrieve 500 gems.

Questions Parents Can Ask:

How many gems do you think you will get in the next handful? Why?

Are the mean and the median close?

How many dives do you think it would take to retrieve 1,500 gems? How do you know?

Challenge:

Try the experiment using two hands to collect gems.

Lollipops in the Bag

Materials:

Paper bags
Red and yellow objects to represent lollipops

Helpful Hints:

Many people inaccurately think the answer to this problem is $1/2$.

The key to finding the correct answer is understanding that there are four possible outcomes; red + red; red + yellow; yellow + red; and yellow + yellow. Three out of the four outcomes include at least one red lollipop.

Answers:

$3/4$ or 3 out of 4 or $12/16$ or 75%
A sample tree diagram is provided; however, student work may vary.
The first bag contains R1 R2 Y1 Y2
The second bag contains R3 R4 Y3 Y4

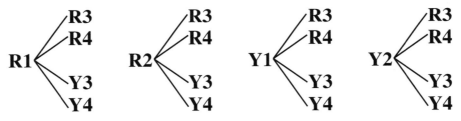

Connections to Math Standards:

Lollipops in the Bag is an activity that allows students to use basic concepts of probability in a simulation of compound events. Students are encouraged to compute probabilities using organized lists and tree diagrams.

Lollipops in the Bag

Math Question: What is the chance of getting at least one red lollipop?

Directions:

1. **Create a tree diagram or organized list to determine the probability.**

> *Each bag contains two red lollipops and two yellow lollipops (four lollipops per bag—a total of eight lollipops). If you reach in the bags (without looking) and take out one lollipop from each, what are the chances that you will get at least one red lollipop?*

2. **Explain the strategy you used to solve this problem.**

Questions Parents Can Ask:

How can you organize all of the possible outcomes?

What are the chances of getting zero red lollipops?

How many ways can you get at least one red lollipop?

Challenge:

Try creating your own "lollipop scenario" involving probability.

Pendulum Swing Experiment

Materials:

    String
    Centimeter rulers
    Scissors
    $1/2$-inch metal washers
    Stopwatches
    Graph paper or scatterplot frame (see page 99)

Helpful Hints:

    Have some washers tied on pre-cut string (60 cm each). Participants can conduct several trials for each string length and find the average number of swings.

Answers:

    Answers will vary; but in general shorter strings will have more swings.

    One possible answer:
        60 cm string swings 20 times
        50 cm string swings 24 times
        40 cm string swings 28 times
        30 cm string swings 32 times
        20 cm string swings 36 times

Connections to Math Standards:

    Pendulum Swing Experiment is an activity that helps students collect, organize, display, analyze, and interpret data. Students are encouraged to see the relationship between two characteristics of a sample on a scatterplot.

Pendulum Swing Experiment

Math Question: Does the length of the string affect the number of pendulum swings?

Directions:

1. Tie a washer to the end of a piece of string. Cut string so that the washer hangs down 60 cm.

2. Hold one end of the string and drop the washer in a manner that allows it to swing like a pendulum.

3. Count the number of swings in 30 seconds. Record the results in your math journal.

4. Cut the string to 50 cm and repeat the experiment. Continue cutting the string by 10 cm and repeating the experiment. Record the number of swings in 30 seconds for each string length (60 cm, 50 cm, 40 cm, 30 cm, and 20 cm).

5. Make a scatterplot of the data collected in this experiment.

Questions Parents Can Ask:

How are the data related? What pattern(s) do you see?

What if you swung the washer for 15 seconds?

If you try the same length string three times, what is the average number of swings? How do you know?

Challenge:

Try different lengths of string and/or swing the washer longer than 30 seconds.

A Day in My Life

Materials:

Drawing paper (8$\frac{1}{2}$ x 11 inches or larger)
Compasses
Protractors
Rulers
Calculators

Helpful Hints:

Display a sample circle graph.

Answers:

A sample table with circle graph is provided, but student work will vary based on the activities and time allotments. Each hour of time will occupy 15° of the circle, since 360°/24 hours equals 15°.

A Typical Day in My Life

Activity	Time	Percent	Degrees
Sleep	8 hrs	33.3%	120°
School	6 hrs	25%	90°
Meals	1 hr	4.2%	15°
Homework	1$\frac{1}{2}$ hrs	6.25%	22.5°
Friends	3 hrs	12.5%	45°
TV/Video	2 hrs	8.3%	30°
Shower/Etc.	2$\frac{1}{2}$ hrs	10.4%	37.5°

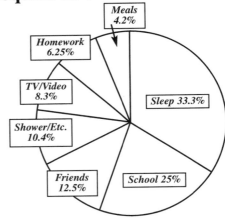

Connections to Math Standards:

A Day in My Life encourages students to apply knowledge of percentages and calculations of the relationship of those percentages to the degrees within a circle in order to represent data.

A Day in My Life

Math Question: How do I determine the size of each section of the circle graph?

Directions:

1. **Generate a table of activities you do during a typical school day. Include an amount of time (which totals 24 hours), the fractional part of the day for the activity, and the percentage of the day spent doing each activity.** Note: To find percent of day divide the time by 24, then multiply by 100. ***Example:***

Activity	Time	Fractional part of day	% of day
Sleep	8 hours	8/24	33.3%
School	6 hours	6/24	25.0%

2. **Use the compass to construct a circle with an 8-inch diameter.**

3. **Add a fifth column to your table to calculate the number of degrees within the circle for each section.** Note: A circle has 360°. ***Example:***

Activity	Time	Fractional part of day	% of day	Degrees
Sleep	8 hours	8/24	33.3%	120°
School	6 hours	6/24	25.0%	90°

4. **Complete the circle graph to represent a typical day.**

Questions Parents Can Ask:

How did you determine the number of degrees for each section of the circle graph?

Were you surprised by the visual display of a day in your life? Why or why not?

Challenge:

How would the graph of a Saturday or Sunday compare to your weekday graph?

Chance for Freebies

Materials:

    Calculators
    Rulers
    Compasses
    Place mat (see page 100)
    Challenge mat (see page 101)

Helpful Hints:

Provide copies of the challenge mat. The challenge mat can be photocopied on the back of the place mat page.

Answers:

Area of the mat: 8.5 in. x 6.25 in. = 53.125 in.^{2}

Probability of winning = area of shape ÷ area of mat
Dessert	2 in.^{2} ÷ 53.125 in.^{2} = .038 = 3.8%
Beverage	1.77 in.^{2} ÷ 53.125 in.^{2} = .033 = 3.3%
Salad	1.5 in.^{2} ÷ 53.125 in.^{2} = .028 = 2.8%
Meal	4.91 in.^{2} ÷ 53.125 in.^{2} = .092 = 9.2%

Probability of winning = area of all shapes ÷ area of mat
Anything 2 in.^{2} + 1.77 in.^{2} + 1.5 in.^{2} + 4.91 in.^{2} = 10.18 in.^{2}
              10.18 in.^{2} ÷ 53.125 in.^{2} = .192 = 19.2%
              or
              .038 + .033 + .028 + .092 = .191 = 19.1%

Connections to Math Standards:

Chance for Freebies is an opportunity for students to understand and apply the concepts of probability in a geometric scenario. Probability is stated as a value from 0 to 1 and is often converted to percentages.

Chance for Freebies

Math Question: What is the probability of winning a free item?

A local restaurant provides a special offer at the conclusion of each meal in an attempt to boost business. The waitperson drops a dinner mint onto the place mat of each customer. If the mint lands on any part of the designated figures, the charge for that item is subtracted from the bill. Note: For this simulation, do not consider the size of the mint.

Directions:

1. Look at the place mat and calculate the probability of a customer receiving each item for free. Base your answer on the dimensions of the mat, 8.5 in. x 6.25 in.

2. Calculate the probability of a customer receiving any item for free.

3. Discuss whether this is a beneficial practice for the restaurant owner.

Questions Parents Can Ask:

*What do you estimate the probability to be?

*Which item do you have the greatest chance of receiving for free? Why?

Challenge:

Sketch a new mat with about a 30% chance of winning a free menu item.

Spinner Maker

Materials:

> Compasses and rulers
> Colored pencils
> Paper clips
> Calculators

Helpful Hints:

> Students will need to recall that a circle contains 360°
> and that all lines on the spinner must pass through
> the center point.

Answers:

> Answers may vary. One possible solution is provided.
>
> | | | |
> |---|---|---|
> | Blue | 10 out of 25 spins = 40% | 360° x .40 = 144° |
> | Yellow | 8 out of 25 spins = 32% | 360° x .32 = 115.2° |
> | Green | 4 out of 25 spins = 16% | 360° x .16 = 57.6° |
> | Red | 3 out of 25 spins = 12% | 360° x .12 = 43.2° |

Challenge Answers:

> Answers may vary. One possible solution is provided.
>
> | | |
> |---|---|
> | Blue section | 216° |
> | Yellow section | 80° |
> | Green section | 40° |
> | Red section | 24° |
> | | 360° |

Connections to Math Standards:

> *Spinner Maker* requires participants to consider the
> theoretical probability of an event first, and then create
> a medium through which the probability could occur
> experimentally.

Spinner Maker

Math Question: What is the probability of spinning each color?

Directions:

1. **Use a compass to draw a circle with a diameter of at least 6 inches in your math journal.**

2. **Use the circle to create a spinner that fits the following desired outcomes:**

> ✔ *It is **least likely** to spin **red**.*
>
> ✔ *There is a **40%** chance of spinning **blue**.*
>
> ✔ *The chance of spinning **yellow** is twice as likely as the chance of spinning **green**.*

3. **Use the paper clip and a pencil to conduct at least 25 spins with the spinner you created.**

4. **Compare your results to the desired outcomes.**

Questions Parents Can Ask:

*How did you determine the size of the blue section on the spinner?

*How did your results compare to the desired outcomes?

*If you completed 100 spins, do you think the results and desired outcomes would be closely aligned?

Challenge:

Create a spinner with a desired outcome of 60% blue.

Chapter Seven:
Additional Tools

Family Math Night Invitation to Parents

Family Math Night Journal Cover

Family Math Night Evaluation Form

How Low Can You Go?

Digits in a Row

Salary Selections

Establishing Order

Spiders and Ants

ABCs and 123s

Pascal's Patterns

All Squared Up

Party With Pentominoes

Newspaper Networks

Try Angles

Cookie Constructions

Deep-Sea Diving

Pendulum Swing Experiment

Chance for Freebies

Family Math Night:
Middle School Math Standards in Action

You are Invited to Family Math Night!

On _____ (date and time)

_____ (school name)

will hold an exciting event called Family Math Night! Students, parents, siblings, and other relatives are invited to attend a fun-filled evening of mathematical pleasure. The intent of Family Math Night is to experience math standards in action as we strengthen the mathematical application, problem solving, and communication skills of students through the power of family interaction.

We encourage you to continue to support your student's mathematical growth through your participation in Family Math Night.

Family Math Night at _____
School Name

_____
Date

Family Math Night:
Middle School Math Standards in Action
——MATH JOURNAL——

Student's Name: _____

Family Math Night:
Middle School Math Standards in Action

_____
(School Name)

_____
(Date)

Did you enjoy the Family Math Night?

Which activity did you like the best?

Which activity do you plan to try again at home?

Would you change anything about Family Math Night?

Place Value Frames

How Low Can You Go?

Round One

Round Two

Round Three

- -

How Low Can You Go?

Round One

Round Two

Round Three

Place Value Names Reference Chart

Tens	Ones	*and*	Tenths	Hundredths	Thousandths
		●			

Number Tiles

1	2	3	4	5
6	7	8	9	+
+	+	+	+	+
−	−	−	−	−

Salary Option Cards

Pay Option A

Earn $1.00 the first hour, $2.00 the second hour, $4.00 the third hour, and so on, doubling the amount earned per hour.

Pay Option B

Earn $12.00 per hour for each hour worked.

Pay Option C

Earn $75.00 per day regardless of how many hours are worked.

Pay Option D

Earn a salary of $450.00 per week regardless of how many hours are worked.

Sequence Cards

A	B	C
(fold)	(fold)	(fold)
$\sqrt{17}$	π	$3^{3/4}$

D	E	F
(fold)	(fold)	(fold)
$\frac{1}{2}$ of 7	4–0.123	8000÷3000

G	H	I
(fold)	(fold)	(fold)
.256 x 10	25% of 12	1.5^2

Blank Sequence Cards

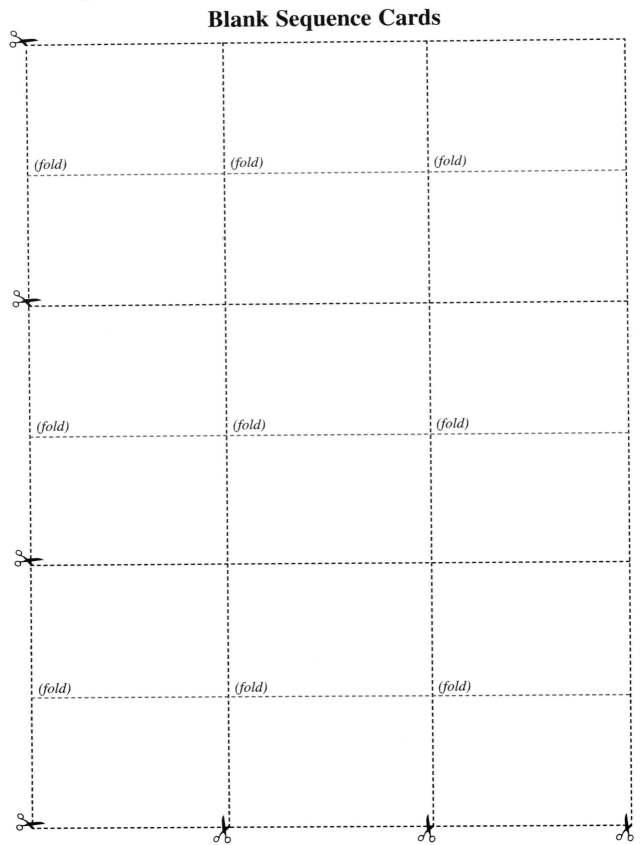

Spiders and Ants Spinner

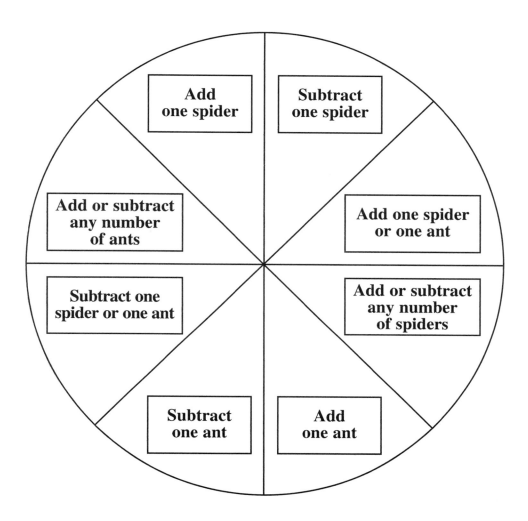

Number Chart

-91	-92	-93	-94	-95	-96	-97	-98	-99	-100
-81	-82	-83	-84	-85	-86	-87	-88	-89	-90
-71	-72	-73	-74	-75	-76	-77	-78	-79	-80
-61	-62	-63	-64	-65	-66	-67	-68	-69	-70
-51	-52	-53	-54	-55	-56	-57	-58	-59	-60
-41	-42	-43	-44	-45	-46	-47	-48	-49	-50
-31	-32	-33	-34	-35	-36	-37	-38	-39	-40
-21	-22	-23	-24	-25	-26	-27	-28	-29	-30
-11	-12	-13	-14	-15	-16	-17	-18	-19	-20
-1	-2	-3	-4	-5	-6	-7	-8	-9	-10

0

1	2	3	4	5	6	7	8	9	10
11	12	13	14	15	16	17	18	19	20
21	22	23	24	25	26	27	28	29	30
31	32	33	34	35	36	37	38	39	40
41	42	43	44	45	46	47	48	49	50
51	52	53	54	55	56	57	58	59	60
61	62	63	64	65	66	67	68	69	70
71	72	73	74	75	76	77	78	79	80
81	82	83	84	85	86	87	88	89	90
91	92	93	94	95	96	97	98	99	100

Equations Strips

$D - J = G$	$B^3 = E$
$I + F = I$	$A \times G = A$
$B+B+B+B=E$	$J + B = E$
$B^2 = I$	$C/H = H$

Pascal's Triangles

Row 0 **1**

Row 1 **1** **1**

Row 2 **1** **2** **1**

Row 3 **1** **3** **3** **1**

Row 4 **1** **4** **6** **4** **1**

Row 5 **1** **5** **10** **10** **5** **1**

Row 6

Row 7

Row 8

Row 9

Row 10

Row 11

Square Grid Paper

Answer Key

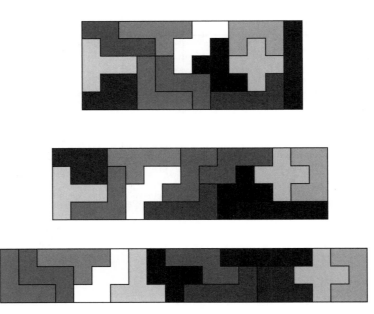

Newspaper Networks Map

START/END

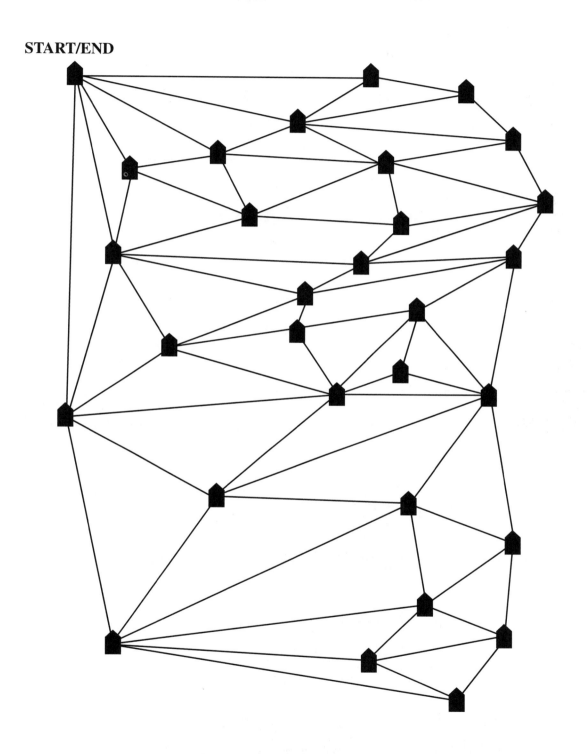

Angle Mat

60 degrees	15 degrees	65 degrees	10 degrees	50 degrees	90 degrees
80 degrees	35 degrees	20 degrees	75 degrees	45 degrees	30 degrees
40 degrees	70 degrees	55 degrees	60 degrees	15 degrees	65 degrees
10 degrees	50 degrees	90 degrees	80 degrees	35 degrees	20 degrees
75 degrees	45 degrees	30 degrees	40 degrees	70 degrees	55 degrees

Cookie Construction Cutouts

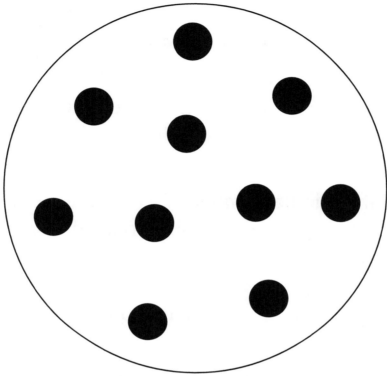

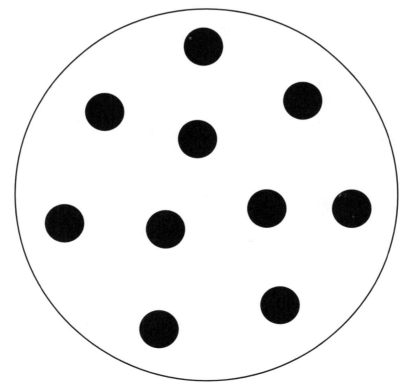

Mean, median, and mode are all types of averages.

Mean: the sum of a set of numbers divided by the number of numbers in the set.

Median: the middle number of a set of numbers when the numbers are arranged from least to greatest (or greatest to least). If there are two numbers in the middle, use the mean of the two numbers to express the median.

Mode: the number that is the most frequent in a set of numbers. In any given set of data, there can be one mode, more than one mode, or no mode at all.

Range: the difference between the greatest number and the least number in a set of numbers.

Scatterplot Frame

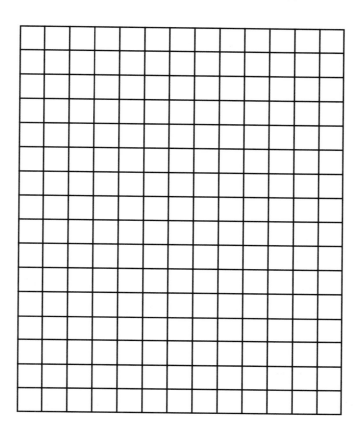

Place Mat

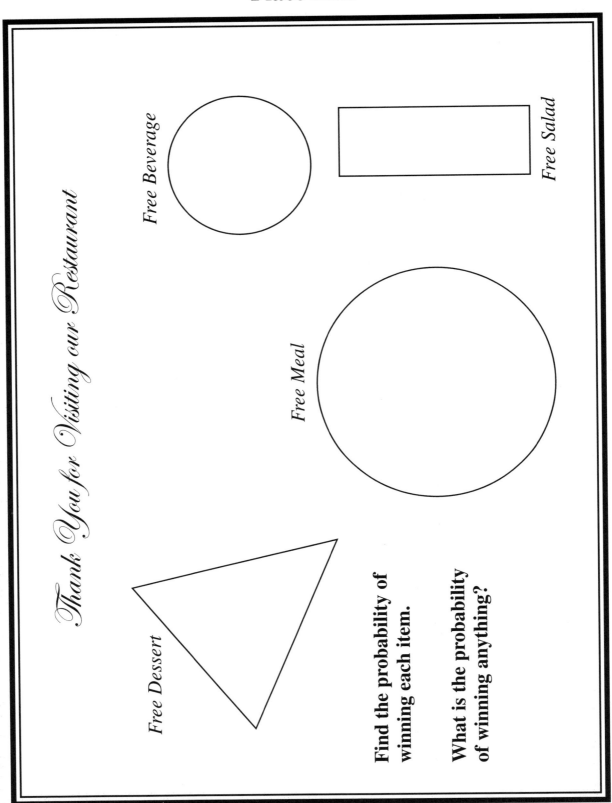

Thank You for Visiting our Restaurant

Free Beverage

Free Salad

Free Meal

Free Dessert

Find the probability of winning each item.

What is the probability of winning anything?

Challenge Mat

Thank You for Visiting our Restaurant!

Design a mat with approximately a 30% chance of winning a free menu item. Show your thinking with words, symbols, and/or equations.

Notes

Notes

Notes